7.95

P9-ELX-065

The Spiritual Life

The Spiritual Life

Evelyn Underhill

MOREHOUSE PUBLISHING
Harrisburg, PA

Published in North America by
Morehouse Publishing

Editorial Office:
871 Ethan Allen Highway
Ridgefield, CT 06877

Corporate Office:
P.O. Box 1321
Harrisburg, PA 17105

Library of Congress Catalog Card Number 84-60646

ISBN 0-8192-1350-0

Fourth Printing, 1994

Front cover: *S. Jerome in his study* by Antonello. Reproduced by
courtesy of the Trustees. The National Gallery, London.

CONTENTS

PREFACE

THE FOUR BROADCAST TALKS which are here reprinted were delivered as a sequel to a previous series by Dom Bernard Clements on the subject of Prayer. They have been revised and slightly expanded for publication; but their informal character has been retained. My object was to present some of the great truths concerning man's spiritual life in simple language; treating it, not as an intense form of other-worldliness remote from the common ways and incompatible with the common life, but rather as the heart of all real religion and therefore of vital concern to ordinary men and women. So far as possible therefore, the use of technical theological terms and direct references to Christian dogma has been avoided; but I believe all that is written here to be in complete harmony with Christian belief. The book is now published in the hope that it may be found suitable for Lenten reading; not only by those who are accustomed to religious literature, but also by some of those whom its language often puzzles and repels. I have already discussed many of the points which are here dealt with at greater length elsewhere; but those who notice this fact are asked to remember the special purpose for which these brief talks were composed.

E. U.

Advent, 1936.

PART ONE

What is the
Spiritual Life ?

"THE SPIRITUAL LIFE is a dangerously ambiguous term; indeed, it would be interesting to know what meaning any one reader at the present moment is giving to these three words. Many, I am afraid, would really be found to mean "the life of my own inside": and a further section to mean something very holy, difficult and peculiar —a sort of honours course in personal religion—to which they did not intend to aspire.

Both these kinds of individualist—the people who think of the spiritual life as something which is for themselves and about themselves, and the people who regard it as something which is not for themselves—seem to need a larger horizon, within which these interesting personal facts can be placed; and seen in rather truer proportion. Any spiritual view which focuses attention on ourselves, and puts the human creature with its small ideas and adventures in the centre foreground, is dangerous till we recognise its absurdity. So at least we will try to get away from these petty notions, and make a determined effort to see our situation within that great spiritual landscape which is so much too great for our limited minds to grasp, and yet is our true inheritance—a present reality here and now, within which our real lives are now being lived. We will look at it through the wide-angle lens of disinterested worship; and put aside those useful little spectacles which bring into sharp focus our own qualities, desires, interest and difficulties, but blur everything else.

There it is, in its splendour and perfection, "shining to saints in a perpetual bright clearness," as Thomas à Kempis said. Not only the subject matter of religion, but also the cause and goal of everything in human life that points beyond the world—great action, great music, great poetry, great art. Our attention to it, or our neglect of it, makes no difference to that world; but it makes every difference to us. For our lives are not real, not complete, until they are based on a certain conscious correspondence with it: until they become that which they are meant to be—tools and channels of the Will of God—and are included in the Kingdom of Spirits which live in, to and for Him alone.

Christians, of course, acknowledge that Will and that Kingdom as the greatest of all realities every time they say the Lord's Prayer; that is, if they really grasp its tremendous implications, and really mean what they say. But so many Christians are like deaf people at a concert. They study the programme carefully, believe every statement made in it, speak respectfully of the quality of the music, but only really hear a phrase now and again. So they have no notion at all of the mighty symphony which fills the universe, to which our lives are destined to make their tiny contribution, and which is the self-expression of the Eternal God.

Yet there are plenty of things in our normal experience, which imply the existence of that world, that music, that life. If, for instance, we consider the fact of prayer, the almost universal impulse to seek and appeal to a power beyond ourselves, and notice the heights to which it can rise in those who give themselves to it with courage and love—the power it exerts, the heroic vocations and costly sacrifices which it supports, the transformations of character which it effects—it is a sufficiently mysterious characteristic of man. Again and again it is discredited by our popular rationalisms and naturalisms, and again and again it returns, and claims its rights within human life; even in its crudest, most naïve expressions retaining a certain life-changing power. No one who studies with sympathy, for instance, the history of religious revivals, can doubt that here, often in a grotesque and unlovely disguise, a force from beyond the world really breaks in upon the temporal order with disconcerting power.

So, too, all who are sensitive to beauty know the almost agonising sense of revelation its sudden impact brings—the abrupt disclosure of the mountain summit, the wild cherry-tree in blossom, the crowning moment of a great concerto, witnessing to another beauty beyond sense. And again, any mature person looking back on their own past life, will be forced to recognise factors in that life, which cannot be attributed to heredity, environment, opportunity, personal initiative or mere chance. The contact which proved decisive, the path unexpectedly opened, the other path closed, the thing we felt compelled to say, the letter we felt compelled to write. It is as if a hidden directive power, personal, living, free, were working through circumstances and often against our intention or desire; pressing us in a certain direction, and moulding us to a certain design.

All this, of course, is quite inexplicable from the materialistic standpoint. If it is true, it implies that beneath the surface of life, which generally contents us, there are unsuspected deeps and great spiritual forces which condition and control our small lives. Some people are, or become, sensitive to the pressure of these forces. The rest of us easily ignore the evidence for this whole realm of experience, just because it is all so hidden and interior; and we are so busy responding to obvious and outward things. But no psychology which fails to take account of it can claim to be complete. When we take it seriously, it surely suggests that we are essentially spiritual as well as natural creatures; and that therefore life in its fulness, the life which shall develop and use all our capacities and fulfil all our possibilities, must involve correspondence not only with our visible and ever-changing, but also with our invisible and unchanging environment: the Spirit of all spirits, God, in whom we live and move and have our being. The significance, the greatness of humanity, consists in our ability to do this. The meaning of our life is bound up with the meaning of the universe. Even though so far the consciousness of this ability and this meaning is latent in the mass of men; yet what an enhancement of life, what devotedness, heroism, and capacity for suffering and for love, what a sure hold upon reality it already produces in those who have felt its attraction, and who respond with courage and without reserve to its demands.

When we consider our situation like that, when we lift our eyes from the crowded by-pass to the eternal hills; then, how much the personal and practical things we have to deal with are enriched. What meaning and coherence come into our scattered lives. We mostly spend those lives conjugating three verbs: to Want, to Have, and to Do. Craving, clutching, and fussing, on the material, political, social, emotional, intellectual—even on the religious—plane, we are kept in perpetual unrest: forgetting that none of these verbs have any ultimate significance, except so far as they are transcended by and included in, the fundamental verb, to Be: and that Being, not wanting, having and doing, is the essence of a spiritual life. But now, with this widening of the horizon, our personal ups and downs, desires, cravings, efforts, are seen in scale; as small and transitory spiritual facts, within a vast, abiding spiritual world, and lit by a steady spiritual light. And at once a new coherence comes into our existence, a new tranquility and release. Like a chalet in the Alps, that homely existence gains atmosphere, dignity, significance from the greatness of the sky above it and the background of the everlasting hills.

The people of our time are helpless, distracted and rebellious, unable to interpret that which is happening, and full of apprehension about that which is to come, largely because they have lost this sure hold on the eternal; which gives to each life meaning and direction, and with meaning and direction gives steadiness. I do not mean by this a mere escape from our problems and dangers, a slinking away from the actual to enjoy the eternal. I mean an acceptance and living out of the actual, in its homeliest details and its utmost demands, in the light of the eternal; and with that peculiar sense of ultimate security which only a hold on the eternal brings. When the vivid reality which is meant by these rather abstract words is truly possessed by us, when that which is unchanging in ourselves is given its chance, and emerges from the stream of succession to recognise its true home and goal, which is God—then, though much suffering may, indeed will remain, apprehension, confusion, instability, despair, will cease.

This, of course, is what religion is about; this adherence to God, this confident dependence on that which is unchanging. This is the more abundant life, which in its own particular language and own particular way, it calls us to live. Because it is our part in the one life of the whole universe of spirits, our share in the great drive towards Reality, the tendency of all life to seek God, Who made it for Himself, and now incites and guides it, we are already adapted to it, just as a fish is adapted to live in the sea. This view of our situation fills us with a certain awed and humble gladness. It delivers us from all niggling fuss about ourselves, prevents us from feeling self-important about our own little spiritual adventures; and yet makes them worth while as part of one great spiritual adventure.

It means, when we come down again to our own particular case, that my spiritual life is not something specialised and intense; a fenced-off devotional patch rather difficult to cultivate, and needing to be sheltered from the cold winds of the outer world. Nor is it an alternative to my outward, practical life. On the contrary, it is the very source of that quality and purpose which makes my practical life worth while. The practical life of a vast number of people is not, as a matter of fact, worth while at all. It is like an impressive fur coat with no one inside it. One sees many of these coats occupying positions of great responsibility. Hans Andersen's story of the king with no clothes told one bitter and common truth about human nature;

but the story of the clothes with no king describes a situation just as common and even more pitiable.

Still less does the spiritual life mean a mere cultivation of one's own soul; poking about our interior premises with an electric torch. Even though in its earlier stages it may, and generally does, involve dealing with ourselves, and that in a drastic way, and therefore requires personal effort and personal choice, it is also intensely social; for it is a life that is shared with all other spirits, whether in the body or out of the body, to adopt St. Paul's words. You remember how Dante says that directly a soul ceases to say Mine, and says Ours, it makes the transition from the narrow, constricted, individual life to the truly free, truly personal, truly creative spiritual life; in which all are linked together in one single response to the Father of all spirits, God. Here, all interpenetrate, and all, however humble and obscure their lives may seem, can and do affect each other. Every advance made by one is made for all.

Only when we recognise all this and act on it, are we fully alive and taking our proper place in the universe of spirits; for life means the fullest possible give and take between the living creature and its environment: breathing, feeding, growing, changing. And spiritual life, which is profoundly organic, means the give and take, the willed correspondence of the little human spirit with the Infinite Spirit, here where it is; its feeding upon Him, its growth towards perfect union with Him, its response to His attraction and subtle pressure. That growth and that response may seem to us like a movement, a journey, in which by various unexpected and often unattractive paths, we are drawn almost in spite of ourselves—not as a result of our own over-anxious struggles—to the real end of our being, the place where we are ordained to be: a journey which is more like the inevitable movement of the iron filing to the great magnet that attracts it, than like the long and weary pilgrimage in the teeth of many obstacles from "this world to that which is to come." Or it may seem like a growth from the childlike, half-real existence into which we are born into a full reality.

There are countless ways in which this may happen: sometimes under conditions which seem to the world like the very frustration of life, of progress, of growth. Thus boundless initiative is chained to a sick bed and transmuted into sacrifice; the lover of beauty is sent to serve in the slum, the lover of stillness is kept on the run all day, the sudden demand to leave all comes to the one who least expects it, and through and in these apparent frustrations the life of the spirit emerges and grows. So those who imagine that they are called to contemplation because they are attracted by contemplation, when the common duties of existence steadily block this path, do well to realise that our own feelings and preferences are very poor guides when it comes to the robust realities and stern demands of the Spirit.

St. Paul did not want to be an apostle to the Gentiles. He wanted to be a clever and appreciated young Jewish scholar, and kicked against the pricks. St. Ambrose and St. Augustine did not want to be overworked and worried bishops. Nothing was farther from their intention. St. Cuthbert wanted the solitude and freedom of his hermitage on the Farne; but he did not often get there. St. Francis Xavier's preference was for an ordered life close to his beloved master, St. Ignatius. At a few hours' notice he was sent out to be the Apostle of the Indies and never returned to Europe again. Henry Martyn, the fragile and exquisite scholar, was compelled to sacrifice the intellectual life to which he was so perfectly fitted for the missionary life to which he felt he was decisively called. In all these, a power beyond themselves decided the direction of life. Yet in all we recognise not frustration, but the highest of all types of achievement. Things like this—and they are constantly happening—gradually convince us that the over-ruling reality of life is the Will and Choice of a Spirit acting not in a mechanical but in a living and personal way; and that the spiritual life of man does not consist in mere individual betterment, or assiduous attention to his own soul, but in a free and unconditional response to that Spirit's pressure and call, whatever the cost may be.

The first question here, then, is not

"What is best for my soul?" nor is it even "What is most useful to humanity?" But—transcending both these limited aims —what function must this life fulfil in the great and secret economy of God? How directly and fully that principle admits us into the glorious liberty of the children of God; where we move with such ease and suppleness, because the whole is greater than any of its parts and in that whole we have forgotten ourselves.

Indeed, if God is All and His Word to us is All, that must mean that He is the reality and controlling factor of every situation, religious or secular; and that it is only for His glory and creative purpose that it exists. Therefore our favourite distinction between the spiritual life and the practical life is false. We cannot divide them. One affects the other all the time: for we are creatures of sense and of spirit, and must live an amphibious life. Christ's whole Ministry was an exhibition, first in one way and then in another, of this mysterious truth. It is through all the circumstances of existence, inward and outward, not only those which we like to label spiritual, that we are pressed to our right position and given our supernatural food. For a spiritual life is simply a life in which all that we do comes from the centre, where we are anchored in God: a life soaked through and through by a sense of His reality and claim, and self-given to the great movement of His will.

Most of our conflicts and difficulties come from trying to deal with the spiritual and practical aspects of our life separately instead of realising them as parts of one whole. If our practical life is centred on our own interests, cluttered up by possessions, distracted by ambitions, passions, wants and worries, beset by a sense of our own rights and importance, or anxieties for our own future, or longings for our own success, we need not expect that our spiritual life will be a contrast to all this. The soul's house is not built on such a convenient plan: there are few sound-proof partitions in it. Only when the conviction—not merely the idea—that the demand of the Spirit, however inconvenient, comes first and IS first, rules the whole

33

of it, will those objectionable noises die down which have a way of penetrating into the nicely furnished little oratory, and drowning all the quieter voices by their din.

St. John of the Cross, in a famous and beautiful poem, described the beginning of the journey of his soul to God:

> " In an obscure night
>   Fevered by Love's anxiety
>   O hapless, happy plight
>   I went, none seeing me,
>   Forth from my house, where all things
>   quiet be"

Not many of us could say that. Yet there is no real occasion for tumult, strain, conflict, anxiety, once we have reached the living conviction that God is All. All

34

takes place within Him. He alone matters, He alone is. Our spiritual life is His affair; because, whatever we may think to the contrary, it is really produced by His steady attraction, and our humble and self-forgetful response to it. It consists in being drawn, at His pace and in His way, to the place where He wants us to be; not the place we fancied for ourselves.

Some people may seem to us to go to God by a moving staircase; where they can assist matters a bit by their own efforts, but much gets done for them and progress does not cease. Some appear to be whisked past us in a lift; whilst we find ourselves on a steep flight of stairs with a bend at the top, so that we cannot see how much farther we have to go. But none of this really matters; what matters is the conviction that all are moving towards God, and, in that journey, accompanied, supported, checked and fed by God. Since our dependence on Him is absolute, and our desire is that His Will shall be done, this great desire can gradually swallow up, neutralise all our small self-centred desires. When that happens life, inner and outer, becomes one single, various act of adoration and self-giving; one undivided response of the creature to the demand and pressure of Creative Love.

THE meaning
of our life is
bound up with
the meaning of
the universe.

PART TWO

The Spiritual Life

as

Communion with God.

THE SPIRITUAL LIFE, THEN, is not a peculiar or extreme form of piety. It is, on the contrary, that full and real life for which man is made; a life that is organic and social, essentially free, yet with its own necessities and laws. Just as physical life means, and depends on, constant correspondence with our physical environment, the atmosphere that surrounds and penetrates us, the energies of heat and light, whether we happen to notice it or not; so does spiritual life mean constant correspondence with our spiritual environment, whether we notice it or not. We get out of gear in either department, when this correspondence is arrested or disturbed; and if it stops altogether, we cease to live. For the most part, of course, the presence and action of the great spiritual universe surrounding us is no more noticed by us than the pressure of air on our bodies, or the action of light. Our field of attention is not wide enough for that; our spiritual senses are not sufficiently alert. Most people work so hard developing their correspondence with the visible world, that their power of corresponding with the invisible is left in a rudimentary state. But when, for one reason or another, we begin to wake up a little bit, to lift the nose from the ground and notice that spiritual light and that spiritual atmosphere as real constituents of our human world; then, the whole situation is changed. Our horizon is widened, our experience is enormously enriched, and at the same time our responsibilities are enlarged. For now we get an entirely new idea of what human beings are for, and what they can achieve: and as a result, first our notions about life, our scale of values, begins to change, and then we do.

Here the creative action of God on a human creature enters on a new phase; for the mysterious word creation does not mean a routine product, neatly finished off and put on a shelf. Mass-production is not creation. Thus we do not speak of the creation of a pot of jam; though we might speak of the creation of a salad, for there freedom and choice play a major part. No two salads are ever quite alike. Creation is the activity of an artist possessed by the vision of perfection; who, by means of the raw material with which he works, tries to give more and more perfect expression to his idea, his inspiration or his love. From this point of view, each human spirit is an unfinished product, on which the Creative Spirit is always at work.

The moment in which, in one way or another, we become aware of this creative action of God and are therefore able to respond or resist, is the moment in which our conscious spiritual life begins.

In all the talk of human progress, it is strange how very seldom we hear anything about this, the most momentous step forward that a human being can make: for it is the step that takes us beyond self-interest, beyond succession, sets up a direct intercourse with the soul's Home and Father, and can introduce us into eternal life. Large parts of the New Testament are concerned with the making of that step. But the experimental knowledge of it is not on the one hand possessed by all Christians, nor on the other hand is it confined to Christianity.

There are many different ways in which the step can be taken. It may be, from the ordinary human point of view, almost imperceptible: because, though it really involves the very essence of man's being, his free and living will, it is not linked with a special or vivid experience. Bit by bit the inexorable pressure is applied, and bit by bit the soul responds; until a moment comes when it realises that the landscape has been transformed, and is seen in a new proportion and lit by a new light. So the modern French woman whose memoirs were published under the name of Lucie Christine was not conscious of any jolt or dislocation of her life, but only of a disclosure of its true meaning and direction, on the day when she seemed to see before her eyes the words "God Only!" and received from them an overwhelming conviction of His reality which enlightened her mind, attracted her heart and gave power to her will. Yet this was really the gentle, long prepared initiation of her conscious spiritual life.

But sometimes the steps is a distinct and vivid experience. Then we get the strange facts of conversion: when through some object or event—perhaps quite small object or event—in the external world, another world and its overwhelming attraction and demand is realised. An old and limited state of consciousness is suddenly, even violently, broken up and another takes its place. It was the voice of a child saying "Take, read!" which at last made St. Augustine cross the frontier on which he had been lingering, and turned a brilliant and selfish young professor into one of the giants of the Christian Church; and a voice which seemed to him to come from the Crucifix, which literally made the young St. Francis, unsettled and unsatisfied, another man than he was before. It was while St. Ignatius sat by a stream and watched the running water, and while the strange old cobbler Jacob Boehme was looking at the pewter dish, that there was shown to each of them the mystery of the Nature of God. It was the sudden sight of a picture at a crucial moment of her life which revealed to St. Catherine of Genoa the beauty of Holiness, and by contrast her own horribleness; and made her for the rest of her life the friend and servant of the unseen Love. All these were various glimpses of one living Perfection; and woke up the love and desire for that living perfection, latent in every human creature, which is the same thing as the love of God, and the substance of a spiritual life. A spring is touched, a Reality always there discloses itself in its awe-inspiring majesty and intimate nearness, and becomes the ruling fact of existence; continually presenting its standards, and demanding a costly response. And so we get such an astonishing scene, when we reflect upon it, as that of the young Francis of Assisi, little more than a boy, asking all night long the one question which so many apparently mature persons have never asked at all: "My God and All, what art Thou and what am I?" and we realise with amazement what a human creature really is—a finite centre of consciousness, which is able to apprehend, and long for, Infinity.

In all the records of those who have had this experience, we notice that there is always the sense that we are concerned with two realities, not one: that while it is true that there is something in man which longs for the Perfect and can move towards it, what matters most and takes precedence of all else is the fact of a living Reality over against men, who stoops toward him, and first incites and then supports and responds to his seeking. And it is through this strange communion between the finite and the Infinite, the seeker and the sought, the creature man and the Creator God—which we may sometimes think of in impersonal terms borrowed from physical nature and sometimes in personal terms borrowed from the language of human love—that the spiritual life develops in depth and power.

Of course, in all this we are trying to think and speak of things which lie at the outer fringe of our consciousness, and of which at best our perception must be dim; for they are almost out of focus, though we know that they are there. So, while we must avoid too much indefiniteness and abstraction on one hand, we must also avoid hard and fast definitions on the other hand. For no words in our human language are adequate or accurate when applied to spiritual realities; and it is the saints and not the sceptics who have most insisted on this. "No knowledge of God which we get in this life is true knowledge," says St. John of the Cross. It is always confused, imperfect, oblique. Were it otherwise, it would not be knowledge of God. But we are helped by the fact that all the responses of men to the incitement of this hidden God, however it may reach them, follow much the same road; even though they may call its various stages by very different names. All mean on one hand action, effort, renunciation of the narrow horizon, the personal ambition, the unreal objective; and on the other hand a deliberate and grateful response to the attraction of the unseen, deepening into a conscious communion which gradually becomes the ruling fact of life.

The old writers call these two activities

Mortification and Prayer. These are formidable words, and modern man tends to recoil from them. Yet they only mean, when translated into our own language, that the development of the spiritual life involves both dealing with ourselves, and attending to God. Or, to put it the other way round and in more general terms, first turning to Reality, and then getting our tangled, half-real psychic lives—so tightly coiled about ourselves and our own interests, including our spiritual interests—into harmony with the great movement of Reality. Mortification means killing the very roots of self-love; pride and possessiveness, anger and violence, ambition and greed in all their disguises, however respectable those disguises may be, whatever uniforms they wear. In fact, it really means the entire transformation of our personal, professional and political life into something more consistent with our real situation as small dependent, fugitive creatures; all sharing the same limitations and inheriting the same half-animal past. That may not sound very impressive or unusual; but it is the foundation of all genuine spiritual life, and sets a standard which is not peculiar to orthodox Christianity. Those who are familiar with Blake's poetry will recognise that it is all to be found there. Indeed, wherever we find people whose spiritual life is robust and creative, we find that in one way or another this transformation has been effected and this price has been paid.

Prayer means turning to Reality, taking our part, however humble, tentative and half-understood, in the continual conversation, the communion, of our spirits with the Eternal Spirit; the acknowledgment of our entire dependence, which is yet the partly free dependence of the child. For Prayer is really our whole life toward God: our longing for Him, our "incurable God-sickness," as Barth calls it, our whole drive towards Him. It is the humble correspondence of the human spirit with the Sum of all Perfection, the Fountain of Life. No narrower definition than this is truly satisfactory, or covers all the ground. Here we are, small half-real creatures of sense and spirit, haunted by the sense of a Perfection ever calling to us, and yet ourselves so fundamentally imperfect, so hopelessly involved in an imperfect world; with a passionate desire for beauty, and more mysteriously still, a knowledge of beauty, and yet unable here to realise perfect beauty; with a craving for truth and a deep reverence for truth, but only able to receive flashes of truth. Yet we know that perfect goodness, perfect beauty, and perfect truth exist within the Life of God; and that our hearts will never rest in less than these. This longing, this need of God, however dimly and vaguely we feel it, is the seed from which grows the strong, beautiful and fruitful plant of prayer. It is the first response of our deepest selves to the attraction of the Perfect; the recognition that He has made us for

Himself, that we depend on Him and are meant to depend on Him, and that we shall not know the meaning of peace until our communion with Him is at the centre of our lives.

"Without Thee, I cannot live!" Whatever our small practice, belief, or experience may be, nothing can alter the plain fact that God, the Spirit of spirits, the Life-giving Life, has made or rather is making each person reading these words for Himself; and that our lives will not achieve stability until they are ruled by that truth. All creation has purpose. It looks towards perfection. "In the volume of the book it is written of me, that I should fulfil thy will, O God." Not in some mysterious spiritual world that I know nothing about;

but here and now, where I find myself, as a human creature of spirit and of sense, immersed in the modern world—subject to time with all its vicissitudes, and yet penetrated by the Eternal, and finding reality not in one but in both. To acknowledge and take up that double obligation to the seen and the unseen, in however homely and practical a way, is to enter consciously upon the spiritual life. That will mean time and attention given to it; a deliberate drawing-in from the circumference to the centre, that "setting of life in order" for which St. Thomas Aquinas prayed.

One of the great French teachers of the seventeenth century, Cardinal de Bérulle, summed up the relation of man to God in three words: Adoration, Adherence,

Co-operation. This means, that from first to last the emphasis is to be on God and not on ourselves. Admiring delight, not cadging demands. Faithful and childlike dependence—a clinging to the Invisible, as the most real of all realities, in all the vicissitudes of life—not mere self-expression and self-fulfilment. Disinterested collaboration in the Whole, in God's vast plan and purpose; not concentration on our own small affairs. Three kinds of generosity. Three kinds of self-forgetfulness. There we have the formula of the spiritual life: a confident reliance on the immense fact of His Presence, everywhere and at all times, pressing on the soul and the world by all sorts of paths and in all sorts of ways, pouring out on it His undivided love, and demanding an undivided loyalty. The discovery that this is happening all the time, to the just and the unjust—and that we are simply being invited to adore and to serve that which is already there—once it has become a living conviction for us, will inevitably give to our spiritual life a special quality of gratitude, realism, trust. We stand in a world completely penetrated by the Living God, the abiding Source and Sum of Reality. We are citizens of that world now; and our whole life is or should be an acknowledgment of this.

"If I climb up into heaven, thou art there: if I go down to hell, thou art there also. If I take the wings of the morning; and remain in the uttermost parts of the sea; even there also shall thy hand lead me; and thy right hand shall hold me."

Consider for a moment what, in practice, the word Adoration implies. The upward and outward look of humble and joyful admiration. Awe-struck delight in the splendour and beauty of God, the action of God and Being of God, in and for Himself alone, as the very colour of life: giving its quality of unearthly beauty to the harshest, most disconcerting forms and the dreariest stretches of experience. This is adoration: not a difficult religious exercise, but an attitude of the soul. "To thee I lift up mine eyes, O thou that dwellest in the heavens": I don't turn round and look at myself. Adoration begins to purify us from egotism straight away. It may not always be easy—in fact, for many people it is not at all easy—but it is realism; the atmosphere within which alone the spiritual life can be lived. Our Father which art in heaven, hallowed be Thy Name! That tremendous declaration, with its unlimited confidence and unlimited awe, governs everything else.

What a contrast this almost inarticulate act of measureless adoration is, to what Karl Barth calls the dreadful prattle of theology. Hallowed be thy Name: not described: or analysed be thy Name. Before that Name, let the most soaring intellects cover their eyes with their wings, and adore. Compared with this, even the coming of the Kingdom and the doing of the Will are side issues; particular demonstrations of the Majesty of the Infinite God, on whom all centres, and for whom all is done. People who are apt to say that adoration is difficult, and it is so much easier to pray for practical things, might remember that in making this great act of adoration they are praying for extremely practical things: among others, that their own characters, homes, social contacts, work, conversation, amusements and politics, may be cleansed from imperfection, sanctified. For all these are part of God's Universe; and His Name must be hallowed in and through them, if they are to be woven into the Divine world, and made what they were meant to be.

A spiritual life involves the setting of

our will towards all this. The Kingdom must come as a concrete reality, with a power that leaves no dark corners outside its radius; and the Will be done in this imperfect world, as it is in the perfect world of Eternity. What really seems to you to matter most? The perfection of His mighty symphony, or your own remarkably clever performance of that difficult passage for the tenth violin? And again, if the music unexpectedly requires your entire silence, which takes priority in your feelings? The mystery and beauty of God's orchestration? Or the snub administered to you? Adoration, widening our horizons, drowning our limited interests in the total interests of Reality, redeems the spiritual life from all religious pettiness, and gives it a wonderful richness, meaning and span. And more, every aspect, even the most homely, of our practical life can become part of this adoring response, this total life; and always has done in those who have achieved full spiritual personality. "*All* the earth doth worship thee" means what it says. The life, beauty and meaning of the whole created order, from the tomtit to the Milky Way, refers back to the Absolute Life and Beauty of its Creator: and so perceived, so lived, every bit has spiritual significance. Thus the old woman of the legend could boil her potatoes to the greater glory of God; and St. Teresa, taking her turn in the kitchen, found Him very easily among the pots and pans.

So here we get, balancing and completing each other, the two first conditions which are to govern man's conscious spiritual life. First, the unspeakable perfection, beauty and attraction of God, absolute in His independent splendour, and calling forth our self-oblivious adoration. And next, the fact that this same infinite God, everywhere present, pours out His undivided love on each of His creatures, and calls each into an ever-deepening communion with Him, a more complete and confident adherence. The completeness of the Perfect includes a completeness of self-giving which yet leaves His essential Being undiminished and unexpressed. He rides upon the floods. It is because of our own limitations that we seem only to receive Him in the trickles. Thus an attitude of humble and grateful acceptance, a self-opening, an expectant waiting, comes next to adoration as the second essential point in the development of the spiritual life. In that life, the spiritually hungry are always filled, if not always with the precise kind of food they expected; and the spiritually rich are sent empty away.

That, of course, is the moral of the story of the Publican and the Pharisee. The Publican's desperate sense of need and imperfection made instant contact with the source of all perfection. He stood afar off, saying "God be merciful, be generous, to me a sinner!" He had got the thing in proportion. We need not suppose that he was a specially wicked man; but he knew he was an imperfect, dependent, needy man, without any claims or any rights. He was a realist. That opened a channel, and started a communion, between the rich God and the poor soul. But the Pharisee's accurate statement of his own excellent situation made no contact with the realities of the Spirit, started no communion. He was dressed in his own spiritual self-esteem; and it acted like a mackintosh. The dew of grace could not get through. "I thank thee, Lord, that I am a good Churchman, a good patriot, a good neighbour." Along those lines there is absolutely nothing doing. No communion between spirit and spirit. No adherence to reality. Osuna says that God plays a game with the soul called "the loser wins"; a game in which the one who holds the poorest cards does best. The Pharisee's consciousness that he had such an excellent hand really prevented him from taking a single trick.

IN the volume of the book it is written of me, that I should fulfil thy will O God.

PART THREE

The Spiritual Life

as

Co-operation with God.

WE COME NOW to the last of Bérulle's three ingredients of a spiritual life: Co-operation. What does that mean? It means that we shall not live up to our call as spiritual creatures unless we are willing to pull our weight. The theological axiom that "Man's will and God's grace rise and fall together" must be translated into practical terms, and given practical effect. More is required of those who wake up to reality, than the passive adoration of God or intimate communion with God. Those responses, great as they are, do not cover the purpose of our creation. The riches and beauty of the spiritual landscape are not disclosed to us in order that we may sit in the sun parlour, be grateful for the excellent hospitality, and contemplate the glorious view. Some people suppose that the spiritual life mainly consists in doing that. God provides the spectacle. We gaze with reverent appreciation from our comfortable seats, and call this proceeding Worship.

No idea of our situation could be more mistaken than this. Our place is not the auditorium but the stage—or, as the case may be, the field, workshop, study, laboratory—because we ourselves form part of the creative apparatus of God, or at least are meant to form part of the creative apparatus of God. He made us in order to use us, and use us in the most profitable way; for His purpose, not ours. To live a spiritual life means subordinating all other interests to that single fact. Sometimes our positions seems to be that of tools; taken up when wanted, used in ways which we had not expected for an object on which our opinion is not asked, and then laid down. Sometimes we are the currency used in some great operation, of which the purpose is not revealed to us. Sometimes we are servants, left year in, year out to the same monotonous job. Sometimes we are conscious fellow-workers with the Perfect, striving to bring the Kingdom in. But whatever our particular place or job may be, it means the austere conditions of the workshop, not the free-lance activities of the messy but well-meaning amateur; clocking in at the right time and tending the machine in the right way. Sometimes, perhaps, carrying on for years with a machine we do not very well understand and do not enjoy; because it needs doing, and no one else is available. Or accepting the situation quite quietly, when a job we felt that we were managing excellently is taken away. Taking responsibility if we are called to it, or just bringing the workers their dinner, cleaning and sharpening the tools. All self-willed choices and obstinacy drained out of what we thought to be our work; so that it becomes more and more God's work in us.

I go back to the one perfect summary of man's Godward life and call—the Lord's Prayer. Consider how dynamic and purposive is its character. Thy Will be *done*—Thy Kingdom *come*! There is energy, drive, purpose in those words; an intensity of desire for the coming of perfection into life. Not the limp resignation that lies devoutly in the road and waits for the steam roller; but a total concentration on the total interests of God, which must be expressed in action. It is useless to utter fervent petitions for that Kingdom to be established and that Will be done, unless we are willing to do something about it ourselves. As we walk through London we know very well that we are not walking through the capital of the Kingdom of

Heaven. Yet we might be, if the conviction and action of every Christian in London were set without any conditions or any reluctance towards this end; if there were perfect consistency, whatever it cost—and it is certain that the cost would not be small—between our spiritual ideals and our social and political acts.

We are the agents of the Creative Spirit in this world. Real advance in the spiritual life, then, means accepting this vocation with all it involves. Not merely turning over the pages of an engineering magazine and enjoying the pictures, but putting on overalls and getting on with the job. The real spiritual life must be horizontal as well as vertical; spread more and more as well as aspire more and more. It must be larger, fuller, richer, more generous in its interests than the natural life alone can ever be; must invade and transform all homely activities and practical things. For it means an offering of life to the Father of life, to Whom it belongs; a willingness—an eager willingness—to take our small place in the vast operations of His Spirit, instead of trying to run a poky little business on our own.

So now we come back to this ordinary mixed life of every day, in which we find ourselves—the life of house and work, tube and aeroplane, newspaper and cinema, wireless and television, with its tangle of problems and suggestions and demands—and consider what we are to do about that;

how, within its homely limitations, we can co-operate with the Will. It is far easier, though not very easy, to develop and preserve a spiritual outlook on life, than it is to make our everyday actions harmonise with that spiritual outlook. That means trying to see things, persons and choices from the angle of eternity; and dealing with them as part of the material in which the Spirit works. This will be decisive for the way we behave as to our personal, social, and national obligations. It will decide the papers we read, the movements we support, the kind of administrators we vote for, our attitude to social and international justice. For though we may renounce the world for ourselves, refuse the attempt to get anything out of it, we have to accept it as the sphere in which we are to co-operate with the Spirit, and try to do the Will. Therefore the prevalent notion that spirituality and politics have nothing to do with one another is the exact opposite of the truth. Once it is accepted in a realistic sense, the Spiritual Life has everything to do with politics. It means that certain convictions about God and the world become the moral and spiritual imperatives of our life; and this must be decisive for the way we choose to behave about that bit of the world over which we have been given a limited control.

The life of this planet, and especially its human life, is a life in which something has gone wrong, and badly wrong. Every time that we see an unhappy face, an unhealthy body, hear a bitter or despairing word, we are reminded of that. The occasional dazzling flashes of pure beauty, pure goodness, pure love which show us what God wants and what He is, only throw into more vivid relief the horror of cruelty, greed, oppression, hatred, ugliness; and also the mere muddle and stupidity which frustrate and bring suffering into life. Unless we put on blinkers, we can hardly avoid seeing all this; and unless we are warmly wrapped up in our own cosy ideas, and absorbed in our own interests, we surely cannot help feeling the sense of obligation, the shame of acquiescence, the call to do something about it. To say day by day "Thy

Kingdom Come"—if these tremendous words really stand for a conviction and desire—does not mean "I quite hope that some day the Kingdom of God will be established, and peace and goodwill prevail. But at present I don't see how it is to be managed or what I can do about it." On the contrary, it means, or should mean, "Here am I! Send me!"—active, costly collaboration with the Spirit in whom we believe.

Consider the story of the call of the young Isaiah. It is a story so well known that we easily take it for granted, and so fail to realise it as one of the most magnificent and significant in the world; for it shows us the awakening of a human being to his true situation over against Reality, and the true object of his fugitive life. There are three stages in it. First, the sudden disclosure of the Divine Splendour; the mysterious and daunting beauty of Holiness, on which even the seraphs dare not look. The veil is lifted, and the Reality which is always there is revealed. And at once the young man sees, by contrast, his own dreadful imperfection. "Woe is me! for I am a man of unclean lips!" The vision of perfection, if it is genuine, always brings shame, penitence, and therefore purification. That is the second stage. What is the third? The faulty human creature, who yet possesses the amazing power of saying Yes or No to the Eternal God, is asked for his services, and instantly responds. "Who will go for us?" "Here

am I! send me!" There the very essence
of the spiritual life is gathered and pre-
sented in a point: first the vision of the
Perfect, and the sense of imperfection and
unworthiness over against the Perfect, and
then because of the vision, and in spite
of the imperfection, action in the interests of the Perfect—co-operation with
God.

The action may be almost anything;
from the ceaseless self-offering of the en-
closed nun to the creation of beauty, or
the clearance of slums. "Here am I!
send me!" means going anyhow, anywhere, at any time. Not where the pros-
pects are good, but where the need is great;
not to the obviously suitable job, which
I'm sure that I can do with distinction;

but to do the difficult thing, or give the unpopular message, in the uncongenial place. "And Moses said, Who am I, that I should go to Pharaoh and bring forth the children of Israel out of Egypt?" But he did it. Indeed, it is a peculiarity of the great spiritual personality that he or she constantly does in the teeth of circumstances what other people say cannot be done. He is driven by a total devotion which overcomes all personal timidity, and gives a power unknown to those who are playing for their own hand or carving their own career.

If we consider the lives of the Saints, we see the strange paths along which they were driven by the Will to the accomplishment of their destiny: how unexpected and uncongenial were the ways in which they were used to bring the Kingdom in and do the Will of God: and how the heavenly Bread which they were given was given to make them strong for this destiny, not because it tasted nice. Great courage and initiative, the hardy endurance of privation and fatigue, the calm acceptance of unpopularity, misunderstanding and contempt, are at least as characteristic of them as any of the outward marks of piety. So too their inner life, which we are inclined to think of as a constant succession of spiritual delights, was often hard and painful. Willingly and perpetually, they prayed from within the Cross, shared the agony, darkness, loneliness of the Cross; and because of this, they shared in its saving power.

The Church is in the world to save the world. It is a tool of God for that purpose; not a comfortable religious club established in fine historical premises. Every one of its members is required, in one way or another, to co-operate with the Spirit in working for that great end: and much of this work will be done in secret and invisible ways. We are transmitters as well as receivers. Our contemplation and our action, our humble self-opening to God, keeping ourselves sensitive to His music and light, and our generous self-opening to our fellow creatures, keeping ourselves sensitive to their needs, ought to form one life; meditating between God and His world, and bringing the saving power of the Eternal into time. We are far from realising all that human spirits can do for one another on spiritual levels if they will pay the price; how truly and really our souls interpenetrate, and how impossible and un-Christian it is to "keep ourselves to ourselves." When St. Catherine of Siena used to say to the sinners who came to her: "Have no fear, I will take the burden of your sins," she made a practical promise, which she fulfilled literally and at her own great cost. She could do this because she was totally self-given to the purposes of the Spirit, was possessed by the Divine passion of saving love, and so had taken her place in the great army of rescuing souls.

That army continues in being, and the call to serve in its ranks would be more frequent and effective if we believed in it a little more: believed in it so much that we were willing to give time and strength to it, and did not draw back when we found that we had to suffer for it. "You will never do much for people, except by suffering for them," said the Abbé Huvelin. In the world of the Spirit that is supremely true. Again and again in the saints we see this saving action of love; but never apart from pain and self-oblation. Real intercession is a form of sacrifice; and sacrifice always costs something, always means suffering, even though the most deeply satisfying joy of which we are capable is mingled with its pain. The thoughts of God are very deep. Bit by bit He moulds us to His image, by giving to us some of His saving power, His redemptive love, and asking our co-operation. From time to time it is our privilege to meet these redemptive souls. They are always people, of course, who love God much, and—as St. Thomas says about Charity—love other people with the same love as that with which they love God; a love which is not satisfied unless it is expressed in sacrifice. When they find someone struggling with temptation, or persisting in wrong-doing, or placed in great spiritual danger, they are moved to a passionate and unconditional self-offering on that person's behalf. If the offering is accepted and the prayer is effective, it means much suffering for the redeeming soul; and presently it appears that the situation has been changed, the temptation has been mastered, the wrongdoing has ceased. When we find ourselves in the presence of such facts as these we are awed and silenced; and our own petty notions of what the spiritual life of man may be and do are purified and enlarged. Cause and effect, perhaps, may not be visible on the surface. But below the surface, there has been a costly victory of love.

We come down from these heights to consider what this complete self-giving to the Spirit can mean in our own quite ordinary lives. St. John of the Cross says that every quality or virtue which that

Spirit really produces in men's souls has three distinguishing characters — as it were a threefold Trade-mark—Tranquillity, Gentleness, Strength. All our action— and now we are thinking specially of action—must be peaceful, gentle and strong. That suggests, doesn't it? an immense depth, and an invulnerable steadiness as the soul's abiding temper; a depth and a steadiness which come from the fact that our small action is now part of the total action of God, whose Spirit, as another saint has said, "Works always in tranquillity." Fuss and feverishness, anxiety, intensity, intolerance, instability, pessimism and wobble, and every kind of hurry and worry—these, even on the highest levels, are signs of the self-made and self-acting

93

soul; the spiritual parvenu. The saints are never like that. They share the quiet and noble qualities of the great family to which they belong: the family of the Sons of God.

If, then, we desire a simple test of the quality of our spiritual life, a consideration of the tranquillity, gentleness and strength with which we deal with the circumstances of our outward life will serve us better than anything that is based on the loftiness of our religious notions, or fervour of our religious feelings. It is a test that can be applied anywhere and at any time. Tranquillity, gentleness and strength, carrying us through the changes of weather, the ups and downs of the route, the varied surface of the road; the inequalities of

94

family life, emotional and professional dis-
appointments, the sudden intervention of
bad fortune or bad health, the rising and
falling of our religious temperature. This
is the threefold imprint of the Spirit on
the souls surrendered to His great action.

We see that plainly in the Saints; in
the quiet steadiness of spirit with which
they meet the vicissitudes and sufferings of
their lives. They know that these small and
changing lives, about which we are often
so troubled, are part of a great mystery;
the life that is related to God and known
by God. They know, that is, that they, and
all the other souls they love so much, have
their abiding place in Eternity; and there
the meaning of everything which they do
and bear is understood. So all their action

comes from this centre; and whether it is small or great, heroic or very homely, does not matter to them much. It is a tranquil expression of obedience and devotedness. As Ornan the Jebusite turned his threshing floor into an altar, they know how to take up and turn to the purposes of the Spirit the whole of life as it comes to them from God's Hand. St. Bernard and St. Francis discard all outward possessions, all the grace and beauty of life, and accept poverty and hardship; and through their renunciation a greater wealth and a more exquisite beauty is given the world. St. Catherine of Genoa leaves her ecstasy to get the hospital accounts exactly right; Elizabeth Fry goes to Newgate, Mary Slessor to the jungle, and Elizabeth Leseur accepts a restricted home life; all in the same royal service.

And we see that all these contrasted forms of action are accepted and performed quietly, humbly and steadily; without reflections about the superior quality of other people's opportunities, or the superior attraction of other people's jobs. It is here that we recognise their real character; as various expressions in action of one life, based on one conviction and desire. Thus there is no tendency to snatch another person's work, or dodge dull bits of their own; no cheapening sense of hurry, or nervous anxiety about success. The action of those whose lives are given to the Spirit has in it something of the leisure of Eternity; and because of this, they achieve far more than those whose lives are enslaved by the rush and hurry, the unceasing tick-tick of the world. In the spiritual life it is very important to get our timing right. Otherwise we tend to forget that God, Who is greater than our heart, is greater than our job too. It is only when we have learnt all that this means that we possess the key to the Kingdom of Heaven.

We have considered that co-operation with the Spirit's action which is to balance our communion with God, as a giving of ourselves to His service, doing some of His work in the world. But there is another and a deeper side: the hidden action of each soul called by God, the effort and struggle of the interior life—what *we* have to do in response to the Love which is drawing us out of darkness into His great light. Even that mysterious communion with God in which we seek, and offer ourselves to, that which we love —in spite of the deep peace it brings—is not without the pain and tension which must be felt by imperfect human creatures, when they contemplate and stretch towards a beauty and perfection which they cannot reach. Still more when it comes to the deeper action, the more entire self-giving, the secret transformation to which that vision of perfection calls us; and the sacrifice, struggle and effort which, sooner or later, this transformation must involve. The Perfection at which the awakened soul gazes is a magnet, drawing him towards itself. It means effort, faithfulness, courage, and sometimes grim encounters if he is to respond to that attraction, and move towards it along the narrow track which leads up and out from the dark valleys of the mind.

I think as I write this of Dürer's wonderful drawing of the Knight, Death and the Devil: the Knight of the Spirit on his strong and well kept horse—human nature, treated as it ought to be, and used as it ought to be—riding up a dark rocky defile. Beside him travels Death, a horrible, doddering figure of decay, saying, "All things perish—time is passing—we are all getting older—*is* this effort really worth while?" On his flank is a yet more hideous fellow-pilgrim; the ugly, perverse, violent element of our mixed human nature, all our animal part, our evil impulses, nagging at him too. In one way or another, we all hear those two voices from time to time; with their discouragements and sneers, their unworthy invitations, their cynical comments and vile suggestions. "Don't forget me, I am your future," says Death. "Don't forget me," says animal man, "I am your undying past." But the Knight of the Spirit does not look at them. He has had his hand-to-hand struggle farther back; and on his lance is impaled the horrid creature, his own special devil, which he has slain. Now he is absorbed in the contemplation of something beyond the picture, something

far more real than the nightmarish landscape through which he must travel; and
because of that, he rides steadily forth
from that lower world and its phantasies
to the Eternal World and its realities.
He looks at that which he loves, not at
that which he hates, and so he goes safely
out of the defile into the open; where
he will join the great army of God. There
we see the spiritual life as humanity is
called to live it; based on the deep conviction that the Good, the Holy, is the Real,
and the only thing that matters, fed and
supported by the steadfast contemplation
of the Holy and the Real—which is also
the Beautiful and the Sane—and expressed
in deliberate willed movements towards
it, a sturdy faithful refusal to look at that

which distracts us from it. Always looking the same way, and always moving the same way: in spite of obstacles, discouragements, mockery and fatigue. "Thou hast made us for thyself, and our hearts find no rest save in thee." But we must be willing to undertake the journey, whatever it may cost.

WE ourselves
form part
of the creative
apparatus of
God.

PART FOUR

Some Questions and Difficulties.

THERE ARE CERTAIN QUESTIONS and difficulties which turn up again and again in relation to the spiritual life. Of these, one of the most fundamental concerns the Nature of God, and the way in which men should think of Him; and in particular, whether Christians can properly use the word Reality and other terms of an impersonal and philosophic sort as synonyms for God. I think that they can and should do so. In religion, where familiar words so easily lose their full meaning for us, it is often valuable to use other words which, though they cannot indeed express the full truth, emphasise other aspects of our great spiritual inheritance. St. Augustine surely answers this question when he says, "God is the only Reality, and we are only real in so far as we are in His order and He in us." St. Augustine was a great Christian. Nothing could exceed the fervour of his personal communion with God. Yet it is the impersonal revelation of a Power and Beauty "never new, yet never old," which evokes his greatest outbursts of adoring joy. The truth is we must use both personal and impersonal language if our fragmentary knowledge of the richness of God's Being is to be expressed; and a reminder of this fact is often a help to those for whom the personal language of religion has become conventional and unreal.

This leads to the next question of importance, which also involves our view of the Nature of God. When we consider the evil, injustice, and misery existing in the world, how can we claim that the ultimate Reality at the heart of the universe is a Spirit of peace, harmony, and infinite love? What evidence can we bring to support such a belief? and how can we adore a God whose creation is marred by cruelty, suffering and sin?

This is, of course, the problem of evil; the crucial problem for all realistic religion. It is no use to dodge this issue, and still less use to pretend that the Church has a solution of the problem up her sleeve.

I would rather say with Baron von Hügel that Christian spirituality does not explain evil and suffering, which remain a mystery beyond the reach of the human mind, but does show us how to deal with them. It insists that something has gone wrong, and badly wrong, with the world. That world as we know it does not look like the work of the loving Father whom the Gospels call us to worship; but rather, like the work of selfish and undisciplined children who have been given wonderful material and a measure of freedom, and not used that freedom well. Yet we see in this muddled world a constant struggle for Truth, Goodness, Perfection; and all those who give themselves to that struggle —the struggle for the redemption of the world from greed, cruelty, injustice, selfish desire and their results—find themselves supported and reinforced by a spiritual power which enhances life, strengthens will, and purifies character. And they come to recognise more and more in that power the action of God. These facts are as real as the other facts, which distress and puzzle us; the apparent cruelty, injustice and futility of life. We have to account somehow for the existence of gentleness, purity, self-sacrifice, holiness, love; and how can we account for them, unless they are attributes of Reality?

Christianity shows us in the most august of all examples the violence of the clash between evil and the Holiness of God. It insists that the redemption of the world, defeating the evil that has infected it by the health-giving power of love—bringing in the Kingdom of God—is a spiritual task, in which we are all required to play a part. Once we realise this, we can accept—even though we cannot understand—the paradox that the world as we know it contains much that is evil; and yet, that its Creator is the one supreme Source and Object of the love that will triumph in the end.

Such a view of our vocation as this brings with it another fundamental question. How are we to know, or find out, what the Will of God is? I do not think that any general answer can be given to this. In clear moral and political issues, we must surely judge and act by the great truths and demands of Christianity; and if we have the courage to do this, then, as we act, more and more we shall perceive the direction of the Will. That choice, cause, or action, which is least tainted by self-interest, which makes for the increase of happiness — health — beauty — peace — cleanses and harmonises life, must always be in accordance with the Will of the Spirit which is drawing life towards perfection. The difficulty comes when there is a conflict of loyalties, or a choice between two apparent gods. At such points many people feel unaware of any guidance, unable to discern or understand the signals of God; not because the signals are not given, but because the mind is too troubled, clouded and hurried to receive them. "He who is in a hurry," said St. Vincent de

Paul, "delays the things of God." But
when those who are at least attempting to
live the life of the Spirit, and have conse-
quently become more or less sensitive to
its movements, are confronted by per-
plexing choices, and seem to themselves to
have no clear light, they will often become
aware, if they will wait in quietness, of
a subtle yet insistent pressure in favour
of the path which they should take. The
early Friends were accustomed to trust
implicitly in indications of this kind, and
were usually justified. Where there is no
such pressure, then our conduct should
be decided by charity and common sense;
qualities which are given to us by God in
order that they may be used.

Next, we are obliged to face the question

as to how the demand of modern psychology for complete self-expression, as the
condition of a full and healthy personal life,
can be reconciled with the discipline, choice
and sacrifice which are essential to a spiritual life; and with this the allegation made
by many psychologists that the special
experiences of such a spiritual life may be
dismissed as disguised wish-fulfilments. In
the first place, the complete expression of
everything of which we are capable—the
whole psychological zoo living within us,
as well as the embryonic beginnings of
artist, statesman or saint—means chaos,
not character. We must select in order to
achieve; can only develop some faculties
at the expense of others. This is just as
true for the man of action or of science as

it is for the man of religion. But where this discipline is consciously accepted for a purpose greater than ourselves, it will result in a far greater strength and harmony, a far more real personality, than the policy of so-called self-expression. As to the attempt to discredit the spiritual life as a form of wish-fulfilment, this has to meet the plain fact that the real life of the Spirit has little to do with emotional enjoyments, even of the loftiest kind. Indeed, it offers few attractions to the natural man; nor does it set out to satisfy his personal desires. The career to which it calls him is one that he would seldom have chosen for himself. It proceeds by way of much discipline and renunciation, often of many sufferings, to a total abandonment to God's purpose which leaves no opening even for the most subtle expressions of self-love.

I come now to the many people who, greatly desiring the life of communion with God, find no opportunity for attention to Him in an existence which often lacks privacy, and is conditioned by ceaseless household duties, exacting professional responsibilities or long hours of work. The great spiritual teachers, who are not nearly so aloof from normal life as those who do not read them suppose, have often dealt with this situation; which is not new, though it seems to press with peculiar weight upon ourselves. They all make the same answer: that what is asked of us is not necessarily a great deal of time devoted to what we regard as spiritual things, but the constant offering of our wills to God, so that the practical duties which fill most of our days can become part of His order and be given spiritual worth. So Père Grou, whose writings are among the best and most practical guides to the spiritual life that we possess, says, "We are always praying, when we are doing our duty and turning it into work for God." He adds that among the things which we should regard as spiritual in this sense are our household or professional work, the social duties of our station, friendly visits, kind actions and small courtesies, and also necessary recreation of body and of mind; so long as we link all these by intention with

God and the great movement of His Will.

So those who wonder where they are to begin, might begin here; by trying to give spiritual quality to every detail of their everyday lives, whether those lives are filled with a constant succession of home duties, or form part of the great systems of organised industry or public service, or are devoted to intellectual or artistic ends. The same lesson is taught by George Herbert's poem:—

" Who sweeps a room as for Thy laws,
    Makes that and the action fine——"

and, in a way that brings it home very vividly to modern minds, by a beautiful letter of Baron von Hügel, which is printed on page fifty-eight of his "Letters to a Niece." This describes how even such a practical activity as packing can be given eternal worth. I do not suggest that this readjustment, this new attitude, can be achieved merely by wishing for it. Nothing which is worth having is as easy as that. It means discipline of thought and of feeling, a more careful use of such leisure as we have; and filling our minds with ideas that point the right way, instead of suggestions which distract us from God and spiritual things. It must also mean some time, even though this may be a very short time, given, and given definitely, to communion with Him; and perseverance in this practice, even though at first we seem to get nothing from it. There are few lives in which there is no pause through the day. We must use even the few minutes that we have in this way, and let the spirit of these few minutes spread through the busy hours. This will also involve expelling from our life those thoughts and acts which are inconsistent with these times of communion. For unless we are prepared to make this the centre of our life, setting the standard to which all the rest must conform, we need not hope for results. We cannot begin the day by a real act of communion with the Author of peace and Lover of concord, and then go on to read a blood-thirsty newspaper at breakfast.

It is this constant correlation between inward and outward that really matters; and this has always been the difficulty for human beings, because there are two natures in us, pulling different ways, and their reconciliation is a long and arduous task. Many people seem to think that the spiritual life necessarily requires a definite and exacting plan of study. It does not. But it does require a definite plan of life; and courage in sticking to the plan, not merely for days or weeks, but for years. New mental and emotional habits must be formed, all our interests re-arranged in new proportion round a new centre. This is something which cannot be hurried; but, unless we take it seriously, can be infinitely delayed. Many people suggest by their behaviour that God is of far less importance than their bath, morning paper, or early cup of tea. The life of co-operation with Him must begin with a full and practical acceptance of the truth that God alone matters; and that He, the Perfect, always desires perfection. Then it will inevitably press us to begin working for perfection; first in our own characters and actions, next in our homes, surroundings, profession and country. We must be prepared for the fact that even on small and personal levels this will cost a good deal; frequently thwarting our own inclinations and demanding real sacrifice.

Here the further question of the relation of spiritual life to public life and politics comes in. It must mean, for all who take it seriously, judging public issues from the angle of eternity, never from that of national self-interest or expediency;

backing our conviction, as against party or prejudice, rejecting compromise, and voting only for those who adopt this disinterested point of view. Did we act thus, slowly but surely a body of opinion—a spiritual party, if you like—might be formed; and in the long run make its influence felt in the State. But such a programme demands much faith, hope and charity; and courage too.